IN THE GARDEN *of*
LIFE

AN ANTHOLOGY OF POETRY AND INSPIRATIONAL MESSAGES

PHYLLIS L. WERNSING

iUniverse LLC
Bloomington

IN THE GARDEN OF LIFE
AN ANTHOLOGY OF POETRY AND
INSPIRATIONAL MESSAGES

iUniverse books may be ordered through booksellers or by contacting:

*iUniverse LLC
1663 Liberty Drive
Bloomington, IN 47403
www.iuniverse.com
1-800-Authors (1-800-288-4677)*

*Because of the dynamic nature of the Internet, any web
addresses or links contained in this book may have changed
since publication and may no longer be valid. The views
expressed in this work are solely those of the author and do
not necessarily reflect the views of the publisher, and the
publisher hereby disclaims any responsibility for them.*

*Any people depicted in stock imagery provided by Thinkstock are
models, and such images are being used for illustrative purposes only.
Certain stock imagery © Thinkstock.*

*ISBN: 978-1-4917-3607-4 (sc)
ISBN: 978-1-4917-3608-1 (e)*

Printed in the United States of America.

iUniverse rev. date: 06/05/2014

Cover Photo by Phyllis L. Wernsing

CONTENTS

TOGETHER AS ONE

Just as the petals of a flower come together to create unique beauty, so shall the creation of past endeavors do the same.

A few years ago I began sharing thoughts and poetry with those around me. I printed booklets and made those booklets available to people that were interested and now, I would like to share three booklets with **you**.

One booklet is called "Walk with Me." Another booklet is called "Flowers on the Vine." I am also including some new thoughts for those who might have any or all of the booklets from past years. I hope you create some thoughts of your own as you read the pages before you.

Come join me in thought as these booklets come together as one **"In the Garden of Life."**

These booklets come together to create thoughts of uniqueness within each of us and help us think differently about the garden we live in.

Psalm 85:8 NRSV
Let me hear what God the LORD will speak, for he will speak peace to his people, to his faithful, to those who turn to him in their hearts.

ASK AND RECEIVE

Many people pray for wisdom. Have you ever prayed for wisdom? Were you given wisdom? Where do you keep your wisdom?

When wisdom is given, it is often placed within one's pocket rather than being used. As you place your hand within your pocket, you may find your wisdom warm and comforting. Or maybe you will find it cool and refreshing. Wisdom comes in many shapes, forms and feelings.

The wisdom given to you is specific **for you** and you can do what you wish with it, but my thought is that if you keep wisdom within your pocket you may have wisdom, but cannot fully absorb the wisdom you have until you use it.

Tell me, where do you keep your wisdom?

Is it safe or do you use it?

Ask and you will receive.

2 Peter 3:14-18 RSV

Therefore, beloved, since you wait for these, be zealous to be found by him without spot or blemish, and at peace. And count the forbearance of our Lord as salvation. So also our beloved brother Paul wrote to you according to the wisdom given him, speaking of this as he does in all his letters. There are some things in them hard to understand, which the ignorant and unstable twist to their own destruction, as they do the other scriptures. You therefore, beloved, knowing this beforehand, beware lest you be carried away with the error of lawless men and lose your own stability.

But grow in the grace and knowledge of our Lord and Savior Jesus Christ. To him be the glory both now and to the day of eternity. Amen

Friendships are made in Heaven and found on earth.

Sometimes when you climb a mountain, the clouds will come and rest on the tops of them. That way you cannot see how tall the mountain is and discouragement will not set in.

BETTER THAN BEFORE

I was upset. Words were spoken that hurt me deeply. The curtain of friendship and sisterhood was tattered and torn. Tears welled up into my eyes and I chose to distance myself from the person that had inflicted the wounds. I needed time to heal. I needed time to sew the torn curtain with threads of understanding and love.

Over the following weeks the truth was made known. I was vindicated, but I still felt hurt and sadness because our friendship can never be as it was before the hurtful incident.

Months passed and my heart still felt the sadness. Then one morning, during my prayer time, I realized that sometimes God allows us to experience things so another might see the truth. I realized that if the incident I spoke of had not happened, the truth would not have been seen by the person that needed to see the truth. If Jesus had not suffered and died for us, we would not have seen the truth of our own lives.

No, our friendship can never be the same, but with the love of my Lord and Savior Jesus Christ, it can be better than before.

Exodus 18:23 KJV
If thou shalt do this thing, and God command thee so, then thou shalt be able to endure, and all this people shall also go to their place in peace.

A CUCUMBER FIELD!

Isaiah 1:8 RSV

And the daughter of Zion is left like a booth in a vineyard, like a lodge in a cucumber field, like a besieged city.

I learned something new today!

I have read the Bible from front to back before, but how wonderful it is to read something and find a new thought among the words of old!

Did you know that a cucumber field is mentioned in the Bible? I do not know why the mention of a cucumber field makes me so joyous, but a cucumber field seems so mundane to be found within the Bible. A cucumber field . . . barely noticed, but still it is there.

How much knowledge of every kind can we find within the pages of the Bible? What little thing might pop out at us from within the words of such a great book? Read the Bible daily. Read the Bible with excitement and find the newness set before you!

Cucumbers . . . I will never think of them the same way again!

DO YOU HAVE CHANGE?

How often do we say: "I have done wrong, but I have paid for it?"

We say that statement quite regularly and we believe it is true. But, can you accept the fact that your sins have been paid for **in full** by the death of Jesus Christ?

So often we expect to be given change concerning our sins. That way we can put the change into our pocket, save it for later and listen to it jingle while we walk. We also get our change out and count it. Then we check to see how much we still owe.

Jesus does not want us to do this! He paid **in full** for you and me. **You** did not pay for your sins. **I** did not pay for my sins. **Jesus Christ** paid for our sins and God does not make change or give refunds! Your bill is paid.
Paid In Full!

Romans 5:8 RSV
But God show his love for us in that while we were yet sinners Christ died for us.

LOOK INTO THE POOL

Proverbs 27:19 RSV
As in water face answers to face, so the mind of man reflects the man.

As I look into the water, I do not see my face clearly.

Waves of time have cast self-doubt before me as a pebble causes distortion upon a calm pool. Many things in life distort my reflection, but there are times when I glance into the eyes reflected within and I am able to smile. When will life be calm within me? When will I reflect God to the world? When will my mind reflect the peace of God and not my humanness?

I find little peace as I gaze upon the pool of my life. How do I know what is required of me Lord?

As my sorrow welled up within me, I felt the presence of Jesus. He quietly said: "When you see My reflection behind you, know that I have calmed the waves of time. Take My hand and I will help you overcome the waves that try to drown you within the pool of your heart. Look into the pool. I am there always."

Thank you Lord for being with me when I go through troubled waters. I also thank you for creating calm pools within my life. Without you I am nothing. Amen.

EACH OTHERS PRESENCE

Dear God,

Hear the tears of troubled hearts today. Receive into heaven, the tears that are shed during sorrow and disappointment. I also lift up to You the joys of laughter. Please receive both tears and laughter into heaven for the wind carries both into Your presence and both are life together unto You.

I ask that You touch the arm of the sorrowful . . . that they may know Your warmth.

Be beside the one that glows with joy for they cannot help but shine from within their hearts.   Be with those that fall somewhere in-between joy and sorrow for they know the presence of both and only You, Lord know where they need to walk.

Be with each of us this day as we walk together . . . knowing nothing of each other's presence. Amen.

1 John 1:6-7 RSV

If we say we have fellowship with him while we walk in darkness, we lie and do not live according to the truth; but if we walk in the light, as he is in the light, we have fellowship with one another, and the blood of Jesus his Son cleanses us from all sin.

FIND ME

I was with a friend. We were talking about those who were standing around us. My friend then said:

"Look into others. There are things you cannot see. Among those things you will find Me. Show them and help them to know I am real. Teach them to look . . . to look and to feel. I am among them. I am there now. If only they would look, they could see My smile."

I will try to help them look for You, Lord Jesus. Amen.

Psalm 103:1 KJV
BLESS THE LORD, O my soul: and all that is within me, bless his holy name!

GOING ON

I came to a resting place and stopped awhile to see.
I laughed, I wept, I hurt.
I touched their lives and they touched me.
I gained from them and they gained from me.
We learned a lot together.
I must go on now to search for something better.

As I thought about the poem above, I realized that we often search for something better. We run here and we run there. Searching. Searching. Searching. But we do not quite find what it is that we search for. When in reality, we are able to find "the something better" right where we are. If we stop running, stop searching . . . Then we may be able to see something better.

Psalm 121:8 NIV
The Lord will watch over your coming and going both now and forever more.

HOW WILL YOU RESPOND?

The angel stood tall and held his trumpet within his hands.

The angel was proclaiming the coming of the Lord and the sound of the proclamation could be heard throughout the earth! All heard the trumpet, but only a few responded to its call. Will you respond?

Did you respond when the trumpet was heard as the world stood beneath the clouds of tomorrow? Did you allow the trumpet to call you to the Lord of the heavens and of the earth or did you walk into the unknown without Him? If you did not respond when the angel called you to service, will you answer the voice of the proclamation now? How will you answer? How will you respond?

Do you hear the trumpet?

The trumpet blows and the voice of the proclamation is of the Lord! So be it.

1 Corinthians 15:51 - 52 NAS

Behold, I tell you a mystery; we shall not all sleep, but we shall all be changed, in a moment, in the twinkling of an eye, at the last trumpet; for the trumpet will sound, and the dead will be raised imperishable, and we shall be changed.

I'LL LAUGH ONCE MORE

My heart cried today.
Its tears I could hear in the things that I wrote.
But I know the sorrow will not forever envelop me.
My heart will laugh once more.
Its laughter will be heard in the words that I say.
Its laughter will be heard on another day.

2 Corinthians 4:8-9 NRSV
We are afflicted in every way, but not crushed;
perplexed, but not driven to despair; persecuted, but
not forsaken; struck down. but not destroyed....

LOOK INTO YOUR HEART

Hebrews 11:6 RSV
And without faith it is impossible to please him. For whoever would draw near to God must believe that he exists and that he rewards those who seek him.

I was reading the scripture above for a Bible Study. As I sat with quietness surrounding me, I heard these words within my thoughts:

"Do you seek him? Do you **earnestly** seek him?"

"Do you **truly** believe?"

"Look into your life. Did you earnestly seek the Creator of Heaven and Earth?"

"Look into your life. Did you truly believe?"

"Have you seen the rewards placed within your life?"

"Now, look into your life once more. Where have you found yourself within its being?"

"Look into your heart."
"When did you disbelieve?"

Lord Jesus, forgive me for my disbelief. Amen.

GOOD INTENTIONS

I often have good intentions, but many of my intentions do not find their way into my day. An example of my intentions is as follows:

I had intended to exercise, but my hip and heel hurt.

I did not sleep much through the night and I woke up tired. My intentions were set aside.

I intended to read my Bible Study lesson, but I did not.

I had intended to be prepared. Instead I went back to sleep and the world passed by my window knowing that my rest was in vain for my thoughts needed to be on paper and dreams are not always needed.

My intentions are good, but unless I act on those intentions… they are only thoughts in my mind.

Lord, I have good intentions. Please help me follow through with them. Thank you for being with me as I go about your day. Amen.

Romans 8:26 NRSV
Likewise the Spirit helps us in our weakness; for we do not know how to pray as we ought, but that very Spirit intercedes with sighs too deep for words.

AS I WALK

As I walk with Thee O'LORD
                    So shall You walk with me.

There are many ways to dream.

There are daydreams; dreams you have at night; and at times, you may simply have a feeling the Lord is walking with you as you go through life.
                    Dare to think. Dare to dream!

On the following pages I will share with you some of my thoughts, feelings and dreams as I walk through life. Come . . . WALK WITH ME.

2 Corinthians 6:16 KJV
And what agreement hath the temple of God with idols? For ye are the temple of the living God; as God hath said, I will dwell in them, and walk in them; and I will be their God, and they shall be my people.

A VISION

I had a dream.

A friend was with me.

I saw several people holding onto something I could not see. The joy on their faces was unmistakable. I smiled as I watched the dream before me. As I turned to my friend, he said: "Happiness is like a vision. Once you have grasped hold of happiness, it disappears . . . vanishing into another dimension . . . to return another time. To make life worthwhile and durable."

Numbers 12:6 RSV

And he said, "Hear my words: If there is a prophet among you, I the Lord make myself known to him in a vision, I speak with him in a dream."

ETERNITY

I saw a baby.

The angels sang with great beauty. The sky was bright with a star that was brighter than any other star in creation.

The baby was born.
A Savior was given.
The world will never be the same!

As the baby came into the world, I could hear his Father say:

"Peace I give to you. My peace I give to you . . . Not just for today, but always. Not as the world gives, but as I give. Our separation is not eternal, for I am there also."

Lord; I thank you for giving us your Son. I thank you for giving us life. And I thank you for being there for us . . . Not just for today, but for eternity! Amen.

Ecclesiastes 3:11 NIV
He has made everything beautiful in its time. He has also set eternity in the hearts of men; yet they cannot fathom what God has done from beginning to end.

STRANGE?

Do we as people
Look at each other
And consider ourselves
As strange as others?
Not I
Said I
In response
To the above.
How could I
Possibly be
As strange
As thee?

Romans 14:10 RSV
Why do you pass judgment on your brother? Or you, why do you despise your brother? For we shall all stand before the judgment seat of God.

A CHILDLIKE FAITH

I have come to realize that my thoughts are often very simple, but also very deep. Isn't that what Jesus talks about when he said we should turn and become like children?

So often we think our thoughts and faith should be complicated. Why? A child will speak in a simple way, but his or her thoughts usually go very deep. Our faith should be that way.

Inside each person is the childlike faith that is a gift to us all. But so often it is kept hidden. We seem to keep our childlike faith (such a special faith) sealed in a can. Occasionally, artificial can openers are used to open our hearts. Then the laughter, joy and enjoyment of simple things can be experienced . . . only to be resealed by us.

Faith can be so simple and so beautiful in a childlike form. This simple faith is within each of us and Jesus is the can opener that is available. **We** need to be the ones to pick up the tool that will open our self-made cans. Jesus will then allow the wisdom of the simple things in life to enter our lives . . . if we will only allow Him to open our hearts.

Matthew 18:3-4 RSV
"Truly, I say to you, unless you turn and become like children, you will never enter the kingdom of heaven. Whoever humbles himself like this child, he is the greatest in the kingdom of heaven."

DIG A GARDEN

There was a time when I felt as if I were in a deep, dark hole and I was unable to find a way out. The hole I found myself in was very fragile, very dark and very deep. In time I allowed Jesus to be with me. Together we filled that hole . . . one spoonful at a time. When the hole was completely full, He said: "By filling the hole slowly and cautiously, it did not collapse upon you."

Those days are only memories now, but I sometimes find myself wanting to pick up a big shovel so I can dig another hole. I find myself digging as fast as I can and as I dig, I can feel the warmth of the sun upon my back. The warmth reminds me that I am not alone . . . for the love of Jesus is with me.

I know that digging a hole and crawling into it are not what Jesus wants me to do. So today, instead of digging a hole, I have chosen to dig a garden. In the garden I will plant all my fear, my sorrow and my disappointments. I will also plant seeds of joy, compassion, love, understanding, patience and knowledge.

I will water my garden each day and then . . .

I will remove the weeds.

Matthew 13:29-30 NIV
"'No', he answered, 'because while you are pulling the weeds, you may root up the wheat with them. Let both grow together until the harvest. At that time I shall tell the harvesters; First collect the weeds and tie them in bundles to be burned; then gather the wheat and bring it into my barn.'"

The promises of God are now…. And forever.

So often I allow things to get in my way and I don't stop to pray…. But not today. Thank you Lord. Amen.

Encourage me Lord…. To do the best I can in every situation that I may encounter today. Amen

EXTRA BAGGAGE

Isaiah 43:25 KJV
I, even I, am he that blotteth out thy transgressions for mine own sake, and will not remember thy sins.

While reading a devotional one morning, I read the scripture above. As I finished reading this scripture, I heard these words within my heart: "Then why should **you** remember them?"

This is so true. God has forgiven me and blotted out my transgressions. Many times **I** do not forget those transgressions. **I** do not blot them out. I carry my transgressions with me like extra baggage taken on a long trip. I carry those extra bags because I think I might need them. In most cases the **extra** baggage could have been left behind and never missed! My journey would have been more enjoyable without the extra weight from the **extra baggage** weighing me down... But I continue to carry the extra baggage because . . . you see, I might need it!

"So why not leave behind the extra baggage you carry today? It will be taken care of in the Lord's Lost and Found Department. The angels will rejoice because you were able to leave your heavy baggage in their care!"

This is what the Lord wants for all his children.

FIND THE DOOR

I was in a place that intrigued me. I felt as if I stood before a giant puzzle. There were many doors and many keys. As I gazed upon the puzzle, everything vanished. A few minutes later the puzzle appeared again and just as before . . . everything vanished. As I stood before the puzzle, a friend opened a door that I could not see and came to my side. He said:

"The keys to the kingdom are yours.

It is up to you to find the door.

Knock and I will answer.

Reach for the keys and you will feel their coolness. You will feel their warmth. Feel them within your hand. Use them with wisdom. Use them with care. They are easy for **all** to hold, but be aware of how you hold them!"

Matthew 16:19 NKJV

"And I will give you the keys of the kingdom of heaven, and whatever you bind on earth shall be bound in heaven, and whatever you loose on earth shall be loosed in heaven!"

THE GREATEST GIFT

To hurt for a friend is a precious gift.
To cry with them is greater.
To laugh with them is the greatest of these three.
To love them is the greatest gift of all.

Mark 12:31 NRSV
*   "The second is this, 'You shall love your neighbor as yourself.' There is no other commandment greater than these."*

HAVE PATIENCE

I was in a crowd of people. Each person was doing their own thing instead of following my direction.

I began to get irritated with them.

As I started to raise my voice, a friend walked into view. He put his hand upon my arm and smiled. He looked toward the crowd of people and said: "Be patient with thyself . . . as you have patience with those surrounding you."

Father in heaven; please help me have patience with myself as well as those surrounding me. Thank You. Amen.

Proverbs 25:15 NIV
Through patience a ruler can be persuaded, and a gentle tongue can break a bone.

IF YOU ASK ME

I stood looking at the cross with a crown of thorns draped over it in preparation for Easter. As I looked at the cross, I felt as if the Lord was asking me to put on the crown. My first thought was that I could not do what Jesus had done and I wondered why He would ask me to wear the crown.

As I thought about my feelings, I realized that we are all called to wear His crown. We are all called to bear one another's burdens.

Finally I was able to answer the question that was placed within my heart. My voice was sorrowful and my heart was heavy. My answer came from within my heart because my mind wanted to answer in a different way. I prayed: "Lord, if You ask me to put on the crown of thorns, I will do so, but I will not be able to walk far . . . because I am weak. Forgive me. Amen."

Give me Your strength Lord because only with Your strength am I able to do the things that You ask of me. Help all of us to wear Your crown and bear one another's burdens. Amen.

Mark 15:17 KJV
And they clothed him with purple, and plaited a crown of thorns, and put it about his head.

JESUS LOVES HER

I was talking with a friend. She was very sad, lonely, hurt and her anger spilled onto all those who befriended her. She seemed to care for nothing . . . not even herself.

I am a fixer and so, I wanted to fix her.

I wanted to make her see she had so much to be thankful for. I wanted her to see how much Jesus loved and cared for her. But no matter what I said or did, she only looked at me and said that God did not love her anymore.

How wrong she is! Jesus loves her very much! Jesus longs to touch her heart. He longs to show her the many ways He has been with her throughout the weeks, months, and years she has closed her eyes to His Presence.

As I prayed for my friend, I heard some words within my heart. The words I heard were not for her. The message was for me.

Within the silence of my heart, I felt the Lord say: "Healing must emerge from the individual." How true it is.

I know I cannot fix my friend. Only Jesus can fix her. If she will open her eyes, I know she will see that Jesus **does** love her.

Lord Jesus, open our eyes that we might see.

Ephesians 2:4 NIV
But because of his great love for us, God, who is rich in mercy, made us alive with Christ even when we were dead in transgressions--it is by grace you have been saved.

KNOCK

I went to a door and knocked. No one answered. I decided the people were not at home. I walked to another door and knocked. The voice of a family pet was heard, but the people of the house were not there either. I started to turn and walk away. As I turned to go, I saw a friend waiting for me. As we exchanged greetings, he gave me a hug and said: "Do not seek perfection because if you seek perfection . . . you will not find it. But if you knock and find a person at the door, surely you have found the image of God."

1 Corinthians 15:49 RSV
Just as we have borne the image of the man of dust, we shall also bear the image of the man of heaven.

THE LORD'S GREAT PLAN

I'll seek the Lord in each new day.
I'll take the time to listen and pray.

I'll try to do the best I can.
In seeking out the Lord's great plan.

I trust He'll show me what path to walk.
I'll try not to stumble on waiting rocks.

He'll open the door as gentlemen do.
And then He'll open a window or two.

I put my life in His great hands.
Trusting Him with all my plans.

Psalm 71:5 RSV
For thou, O Lord, art my hope, my trust, O Lord from my youth.

MAYBE . . .

As I traveled a lonely road, the sun poked its nose over the horizon. The sun was shining brightly and it made me smile as I felt its warmth on my arm.

Suddenly I felt like a child and found myself saying: "Hi Mr. Sun! Or are you Ms. Sun?" The child within me continued the conversation. "You look great today! I see you have your best clothes on and you even fluffed your hair this morning. You look bright and shiny."

"Your rays will touch many hearts today. You are truly beautiful for the world to see. Have a good day! Oh, I almost forgot, please say hi to God for me! Thank you! Good bye for now!"

Now, you might think I'm a little strange, but maybe we should all take time to become like a child and say hi to the sun! It might do our hearts some good!

Next time I think I will dance with the flowers. Maybe I will sing with the wind.

Maybe I will fly a kite.

Maybe . . .

Lamentations 3:22-23 NAS
The Lord's lovingkindnesses indeed never cease, For His compassions never fail. They are new every morning; Great is Thy faithfulness.

A LITTLE MORE STRANGE

Strange?
Do we as people
Look at each other
And consider ourselves
As strange as others?
Not I!
Say I!
In response
To the above.
How could I
Possibly be
As strange
As thee?
O Lord,
Please,
Open my eyes
That I might see
I'm just as strange
As he might be.
Yes,
Together we'll stand.
Divided we'll fall.
Without You Lord
Not at all!

Romans 14:12 RSV
So each of us shall give account of himself to God.

NO DARKNESS

I was in a dark place. I felt afraid and sorrow was within my heart. I grieved for those around me, but I could not see them. I did not know why I was in such a dark place. In fear I called for The One I trusted. He took my hand and said:

"Now walk with me into my world where fear cannot be felt because **there is no darkness**."

And so . . .

> A new person emerged from the sorrow.
> Light descended upon darkness and life
> came forth upon wings of joy!

Thank you Lord for bringing me out of my darkness into Your Light. Amen.

1 John 2:8 RSV
Yet I am writing you a new commandment, which is true in him and in you, because the darkness is passing away and the true light is already shining.

OPPORTUNITIES

I sat listening to a bright young pastor deliver his sermon. I do not remember every part of his sermon, but one sentence caught my attention. He said: "Not everyone will have the opportunity to do great things, but everyone will have the opportunity to do small things in great ways."

That one sentence is so true. Not all of us will write a great symphony. Not all of us will swim the English Channel. Not all of us will be president or climb Mount Everest. And none of us will die on a cross.

There are many things we probably will not do, but there are many things we can do. We can listen to the symphony and then share it with someone that cannot hear. We can cheer as the swimmer reaches his goal and then ask a lonely person to go with us to water aerobics. We can pray for the leaders of our country and then vote. We can walk up the nearest hill as if it were the tallest mountain in the world while we hold onto the hand of a small child. Thankfully, Jesus died on the cross so we do not have to.

Yes, we have many opportunities to do small things in great ways.

Thank you Scott for sharing this thought with all of us. Amen.

Galatians 6:10 KJV
As we have therefore opportunity, let us do good unto all men, especially unto them who are of the household of faith.

OFF KEY

It was Christmas. The children of my church put on a Christmas program. They sang eagerly, but one small child sang a little off key. As I watched the children, I smiled. Even though one was not quite in tune, I found delight in the program.

Just as that one child was a little off key, we can also find ourselves a little off key and like the singing child, we are not embarrassed because we are not aware of it. We continue with enthusiasm and excitement, thinking we are in tune with the other people around us.

Even though we may be a little off key, our words are still heard. A loving Father listens with patience and love. A faint smile appears on his face and there is a gleam in his eye. He knows with time and love the person singing off key will grow to show his full potential.

There are no doors closed to what we can accomplish with a great and loving Father that listens . . . even when we sing off key.

Jeremiah 29:11 NIV
"For I know the plans I have for you," declares the Lord, " plans to prosper you and not to harm you, plans to give you hope and a future."

THE ROADS WE TRAVEL

While on a trip to see our son, I noticed significant changes in the roads. We crossed from one county to another county. We crossed from one state to another state. As we crossed these county and state lines, I noticed some roads along the way were narrow and neglected. Others were groomed to perfection. I also realized, at times, the landscape was green and full of vibrant color. At other times, I wondered how anything could exist in such a barren and desolate land. Although the contrast was obvious . . .

I found beauty in both.

Isn't it amazing how the roads we travel in life are often like the roads we travel in our country?

Look for the beauty.

Beauty can be found in both.

1 Timothy 4:4 NAS
For everything created by God is good, and nothing is to be rejected, if it is received with gratitude.

A SUNBEAM

There's a sunbeam in my kitchen.
It smiles across the floor.
The only time it starts to frown
Is when I close the door.

It dances to the music
Played within my home.
It keeps the beat to little feet
And sings its special song.

It brings a smile to each small child.
And then to grownups too.
So when you see the sunbeam,
You know that God loves you.

The sunbeam plays a little while.
It giggles and it laughs.
And then it goes to play next door.
Oh my, the day has passed!

Yes, when you see the sunbeam
Dancing across the floor.
Open wide the windows.
And open up the doors.

It's come to dance and bring a smile.
To sing a song or two.
The sunbeam in my kitchen
Has come to play with you!

Exodus 32:6 KJV
And they rose up early on the morrow, and offered burnt offerings, and brought peace offerings; and the people sat down to eat and to drink, and rose up to play.

Stir me Lord.
For I have been asleep…. Too long a time.

The image of Jesus can be seen on an empty cross for those who seek Him.

The words I hear from the Lord is music to my ears and peace to my heart.

THEY BECAME ONE

It was Easter and I was at an evening candlelight service.

This was a beautiful service. I found myself fascinated with the candle I held in my hand. The wax was dripping down the side of my candle and made an interesting shape. As the candle glowed in the darkness, the wax dripping down its side, resembled tears.

The drips merged into one beautiful creation.

Before my eyes, the wax molded itself into an image of someone praying. The person kneeled over another mound of wax which resembled tears . . . or maybe it represented our sins.

The image I held within my hands took on the shape of someone I knew . . . the image of Mary, the mother of Jesus. The mound of tears also took on a shape that I knew . . . the image of the cradle Jesus was placed into after Mary gave birth to Him. Both shapes were familiar to me.

What a beautiful sight to behold!

I saw a new creation in the darkness which was illuminated by the soft light of my candle. As I gazed upon the creation before me, I heard these words within my heart:

"Tears were placed beneath the cross and as the day turned into night, the blood that was shed for all sin merged with those tears . . . and they became one."

Hebrews 5:7 NAS
In the days of His flesh, He offered up both prayers and supplications with loud crying and tears to the One

able to save Him from death, and He was heard because
of His piety.

We must help each other to ensure the quality of life that ensures happiness and life for all.

Sometimes, after experiencing the worst, we are able to **feel** the best. For we have known both.

Small adjustments can sometimes cause large benefits, but they can also create messes. Choose wisely.

THE PRISON YARD

I looked into the prison yard and among the men I saw a familiar face. I saw a man with forgiveness in His eyes and love for those who recognized Him.

Many times we think that those in prison created their own problems. We sometimes feel afraid of them. We may think that they got what they deserved. There are many more statements I can make and all of those statements may be true. But Jesus said to visit the people in prison. So, what shall we do about this challenge set before us? Shall we ignore the whole thing?

Do you think it will go away? Somehow I don't think it will go away. It will be there every time we pick up our Bible and most of us will just turn the page.

I wonder what Jesus would do?

Jesus knows visiting people in prison is a hard thing for us to do. Visiting prisons make most people uncomfortable. Many times I don't want to think about the whole situation, but Jesus thinks about it more often than we would like to admit. He thinks about the people in prison enough to tell us to visit them. Jesus knew how easy it would be for us to pretend that those in prison are fine. They did the crime. Now they must do the time and we don't have to be bothered with them. How sad. Jesus knew we needed to be told that he cares for his lost children. Yes, Jesus can be seen walking among the prison walls.

I wonder how many will recognize Him?

Matthew 25:39-40 NRSV

"And when was it that we saw you sick or in prison and visited you?' And the king will answer them, 'Truly I tell you, just as you did it to one of the least of these who are members of my family, you did it to me.'

The song of my heart sings with joy and dances with heavenly music. Come…. Dance with me for the day is young and the music soothes the soul.

The spirit of those who have gone before us is with us also. Feel their spirit from years gone by as well as those near for they are as near as those gone by.

Beware of pride for it is the destroyer of all who embrace it too tightly.

THE EIGHTS?

We all have things we wrestle with within our lives.
Some people wrestle with tougher things than others, but we all wrestle with things we see and feel.

As I sat in prayer, the following words disturbed my heart. I did not know what they meant, so I asked. The scripture below was given to me.

Luke 11:24 - 26 NKJV
"When an unclean spirit goes out of a man, he goes through dry places, seeking rest; and finding none, he says, 'I will return to my house from which I came'. "And when he comes, he finds it swept and put in order. "Then he goes and takes with him seven other spirits more wicked than himself, and they enter and dwell there; and the last state of that man is worse than the first."

I feel we all need to be careful when we sweep our homes. We need to fill those empty places with Jesus or they may be filled with unwanted things that cause us sorrow and pain. This is what I heard within my heart and yes . . . it disturbed me!

Cry with me.

The tears will flow like rivers and hearts will break in two. The rest will be short and savage. Beasts will endure much pain. The sky will be bright with sorrow. The eights will reign no more. The beginning becomes the end and the rainbows are broken. The valleys have shadows with rivers running cold. The hurt remains even after the end and the pieces are glued back together with the blood of those before it.

I will ask no more questions concerning the eights Lord . . . for I fear you might tell me more and I wish to remain safe. Forgive me. Amen.

The Light creates warmth for those who seek it. Seek the Light and warm up to the warmth created by eternity.

So, What **is** time? What is a day, a month, a year? It is nothing in God's time. Use time wisely.... For time moves quickly within the folds of time.

USE YOUR LOVE

A friend and I were looking at something beautiful. It was soft, warm and gentle. It made me feel wonderful. I wanted to stay where I was forever. I asked my friend to tell me about this wonderful feeling. He said:

"Love is to be used. Keep your love and it will get stale and brittle. Use it and your love will stay soft and gentle."

I will use the love that You have given me Lord. Thank You for such a wonderful gift. Amen.

Matthew 16:27 NKJV
For the Son of Man will come in the glory of His Father with His angels, and then He will reward each according to his works.

ANOTHER DAY

The Lord gave me another day.
To see what good I can find in it.
To love those around me.
To seek His divine purpose.
To hear the birds sing.
To feel the warmth of His sun.
To feel His presence in my pain.
And then to laugh again.

Psalm 25:17 RSV
Relieve the troubles of my heart, and bring me out of my distresses.

BEYOND THE MOUNTAIN

A stream flows gently through a field of wild flowers. The pasture gently turns into a rolling hill. Mountains begin to challenge your ability. The steep, rugged terrain remains for you to climb. The rocks catch your foot and cause you to stumble. You pick yourself up and continue climbing the mountain. When you have reached the top, the view is breathtaking and you can see far beyond the beauty set before you. Accomplishing the task at hand makes you smile, but remember . . .

Looking toward that mountain is a beautiful sight.

Looking beyond it is of God.

Psalm 36:5 RSV
Thy steadfast love, O Lord, extends to the heavens, thy faithfulness to the clouds.

AM I NORMAL?

I sat talking quietly with a friend. My friend reflected upon what I was saying. In response, he spoke these words:

"You are a normal person and your normalness is heard. For your normalness screams from the tallest mountain and yet, in its normalness, it is unique in its own way."

Thank you Lord for allowing us to be ourselves. Amen.

1 Corinthians 12:27 NIV
Now you are the body of Christ, and each one of you is a part of it.

ART AND PRAYER

I went to a creative workshop about art and prayer. During this refreshing day I wrote what was placed within my heart. I would like to share these thoughts with you. My day is entitled: Thoughts Along the Path of a Beautiful Day.

The Lioness shall seek the lamb that has come into her presence.

(Right after I wrote these words, I looked up and saw the Lioness within the wood creation upon the coffee table. I feel the Lord smiles as we see the beauty of all His creation . . . the beauty of the female which He has created in beauty.)

Into the life of those who seek . . . so shall they see the Light surrounding each who seek within themselves.

Can you see anything?

Walk into the beauty set before you and see. Do you see anything?

Do you see the blind man? The homeless?

Walk the path of sunshine among the trees. Do you see a broken limb?

Do you see the strength of the Lion? Look farther. Do you see the life that the death of One brings to another?

Can you see anything?

Can you see the song set within the warmth of creation? The song of beauty and truth?

Can you see?

Can you hear the strength of life touching all that surrounds you?

For life is not but one, but many touching each other as they walk among the clouds that support their purpose.

Can you see?

Can you hear?

Can you feel the presence of life set before you?

✝✝✝

The feather gently moves on the coolness of the wind . . . meeting as they dance within the presence of God. Dance with God as the feather dances with the wind.

The music within your heart longs to sing as the bird in the tree sings unto the sun rising in the morning sky. The rays of song reach upward to the heavens of life and the heavens return it unto the earth with warmth. The clouds reach within the spaces known only unto you, but the God Rays of the sun reflect through the clouds and make your smile reflect its beauty.

✞✞✞

A line is not straight if it is bent into a circle which connects itself unto itself . . . encompassing all that is within its presence. The circle is what you see unless you straighten it and carry it as a straight and rigid line. Bend like the reed beside the water and you will not break upon the wind and heat of the seasons of drought.

Bend. Sway. Move like the dance of life.

✞✞✞

Gaze upon something that does not gaze back at you. Is it you looking upon yourself . . . longing to reach out from within and gaze upon a life of love and truth? Look unto the cross and see . . . who is gazing back at thee?

The thunder rolled across the sky in sight and sound . . . awakening the Spirit within.

Step into the thunder.

Take hold of the wind and shine before life as lightning upon a dark and sleeping world.

Do you read words or do you see words? Do you walk into the things you see and feel? Within each creation is a life of its own . . . no matter if it was created with human hands or created by the being of God within the creation. God created both.

Within the business within life . . . solitude can be found. Look to see, where is your solitude beneath the sky and the wind? Beneath life and death created for all to see? Where is solitude when you turn to look at life set before you? Look. See. Solitude is created within life and often is not found until death. Look. See. Is solitude beyond your beauty or is it a part of your beauty? Solitude is found in both. Look. See.

While in prayer, I asked the Lord: "Where would you have me go?"

Within my heart and mind I heard these words: "Go into the crevices of life where most would not have the strength to trod. Find there the beauty that your eyes shall see and bring it out of the unknown for others to see."

Lord, where are my crevices? Are they within me or shall I find them in the world that You have created? Possibly. Just possibly . . . I shall find crevices within both and I will walk with You as You show me the beauty created in Your likeness. You, Lord, have created all that my eyes see. You have created all that my heart touches. Lead me Lord that I might be. Amen.

We were asked to find a rock.

I picked up a rock and looked within it.

I saw a mountain.

On the mountain I saw the sun shining for all that climbed it.

Within my heart I heard these words:

"The rock you have chosen has been run over by many cars coming into the sanctuary. The rock has survived . . . the beauty within is revealed to the sun that has seen its beauty before your hands have touched it."

I created a watercolor painting. Its meaning became known to me.

This is what I heard within my heart: "From earth's inner space you shall cast creativeness unto the echoes of time and it shall return as beauty upon the wind." Thank you Lord. Amen.

UPON A TEAPOT LID

A bird sitting upon a teapot lid looking out a window.
What does he see?
What does he feel sitting on a teapot
lid looking out a window?
Does he long to be free?
Does he long to be real?
As he sits upon a teapot lid.
Looking out a window.

Psalm 102:7 NIV
I lie awake; I have become like a bird alone on a roof.

(Or maybe a teapot lid?)

DO THIS FOR ME

I sat talking with a friend. With love and understanding, He said:

"Stop fighting each other and strive for love and understanding **of** one another. Do this for Me because together; in love and harmony, you will stand.

Apart, you will crumble and fall defeated."

Colossians 3:14 NAS
And beyond all these things put on love, which is the perfect bond of unity.

YOUR SHADOWS

I came to the Lord in prayer. Within my heart I heard these words:

"Remember I conquered the darkness that engulfed the entire world. Through Me you conquered your battle and stand in My light. My light alone can conquer all darkness. The darkness bows to Me! The darkness is brought to its knees each time one of my people turns in the direction of the Full Light. I am the Full Light! There are no shadows in My Light!"

"Just as I have said that the rainbow has no shadows, so it is with My Light. You see a small portion of my reflected light in a rainbow. I show you many times over how I work and feel . . . and still you need My reassurance that I love you each day! It is good that you need Me, but be careful of **your shadows**."

Forgive me Lord. At times my shadows seem so dense, but I will try to hold Your Light before me. Amen.

1 Chronicles 29:15 NRSV
For we are aliens and transients before you, as were all our ancestors; our days on the earth are like a shadow, and there is no hope.

COLORS

A storm had passed. As I watched it travel to a distant place, a rainbow filled the sky. The rainbow was breathtaking. I found myself watching the rainbow until it faded into the heavens. As I marveled at the rainbow's beauty, I felt the presence of a friend. He smiled and said:

"When you see a rainbow within a cloud filled sky, look for an Angel sitting nearby. He collected the tears of all those that cry. He took all those tears and painted the sky. A reminder from Jesus as to why He died. He painted those colors for you and me. He painted those colors for the world to see."

Isaiah 25:8 RSV
He will swallow up death forever, and the Lord GOD will wipe away tears from all faces, and the reproach of his people he will take away from all the earth; for the Lord has spoken.

A WARM GLOW

God's love is like the sun shining on a person wanting a tan. The sun's warmth cannot be seen by our eyes, but it **can** be felt. The results are often seen upon those who seek its warmth.

Just as a tan is produced by the sun, so does God's love produce a warm glow inside the ones that seek Him. Then, if we look closely, we will see the glow reflecting outside of them as well

I pray all of us will bask in the warmth of God's love. We can all use a beautiful tan! Amen.

2 Corinthians 3:18 RSV
And we all, with unveiled face, beholding the glory of the Lord, are being changed into his likeness from one degree of glory to another; for this comes from the Lord who is the Spirit.

FLOWERS ON THE VINE

When we take time and listen to the Lord, His thoughts can bloom like flowers on a vine. His thought may begin as a bud begins. Then with care and attention, the bud may blossom into a creation of great beauty.

Take time to listen, no matter how small that time may be. See His glorious beauty. Nurture it with love and understanding.

Take time for the Lord!

Listen! His thoughts are like FLOWERS ON THE VINE.

John 15:5 NRSV

I am the vine, you are the branches. Those who abide in me and I in them bear much fruit, because apart from me you can do nothing.

THE ONE THAT SINGS

I sat in a lonely place and held sorrow within my hands. A friend called my name. When he found me, he sat and gazed upon the sorrow that I held and then he said:

"From age to age time has touched the edges of the universe and the mountains held their heads high in the midst of the storms. The waters made the trees stand tall and the flowers bloom."

"Despair does not claim the universe because the universe belongs to The One that sings upon the wind and His joy vibrates throughout the heavens."

As I tossed my sorrow into the wind, a song filled my heart.

Thank you Lord. I will try to hear Your Song within the wind. Amen.

Exodus 15:2 NAS
The Lord is my strength and song, And he has become my salvation; This is my God, and I will praise Him; my father's God, and I will extol Him.

LIFE SMILED

Life
Stirred
Within the gentle earth.
Life was born.
With joy and anticipation,
Life reached toward the
Warmth of the sun
And smiled.

Job 8:19 KJV
　　Behold, this is the joy of his way, and out of the earth shall others grow.

VARIETY

I sat quietly. I heard these words within my heart: "There is variety in much of my creation. That is because no one can put me into a box. I created everything and I can be seen in everything."

"Where one sees me, another will not see me. One might see me playing among the clouds and another may find me praying in my garden. Still, another may see me skip a stone across still waters. I cannot be contained in anything or anyone place."

1 Kings 8:27 NKJV
"But will God indeed dwell on the earth? Behold, heaven and the heaven of heavens cannot contain You. How much less this temple which I have built!"

MARY

Mary. Oh Mary. I can feel your pain.
I feel you long to go back again.

To hold your baby close to your breast.
To feed him, rock him and give him some rest.

You sing the lullabies of ages past.
Your love is so tender and forever will last.

You'll try to show him the way that is good.
And shield him from pain . . . If only you could.

You talk to him softly and hold his small hand.
You gaze at his face. You understand.

You were given a baby many years ago.
A baby I feel you are longing to hold.

Yes Mary, I can feel your pain today.
If only, I could find some words to say.

But if you went back to hold him once more.
Your precious baby. The son you adore.

You'd gaze at his face and hold his small hand.
You'd look to the heavens. You'd understand.

Matthew 1:21 KJV

And she shall bring forth a son, and thou shalt call his name JESUS: for he shall save his people from their sins.

GOOD IS NOT BAD

I sat with chaos swirling around me. In the distance I saw a beautiful lake with trees, flowers and fish topping the water. A friend stepped gently between the things that swirled around me. We sat quietly for a while and then he said:

"Focus on the good things in life . . . or do something about the bad. Then when you have done something about the bad, it becomes good and the good is not bad."

Psalm 106:1 KJV
PRAISE YE the Lord. O give thanks unto the Lord; for he is good: for his mercy endureth forever.

TO A FRIEND

As I looked at the lilies in the garden, I saw your face. Your eyelashes glistened with dew. The flowers around you were glistening too. Then the sun rose high in the sky and dried the dew within your eyes.

Psalm 30:5 NKJV
For His anger is but for a moment, His favor is for life; Weeping may endure for a night, But joy comes in the morning.

AN OVERCOAT

As I sat thinking about a friend one day, I heard these words within my heart:

"I put your burdens on like an overcoat that goes down to my ankles. I will gladly wear them if you will allow me to keep them. Do not take them away from me. For then I will be naked in front of those before me. They will be able to see all my faults and my sadness will become known to those who are able to recognize me."

"But if you are not able to give me your burdens, I will understand. If you choose to reclaim them, I will stand before those who recognize me and I will not be ashamed."

Although Jesus is faultless, He carries our faults with Him as if they were a lining in an overcoat. For those who recognize Him, His nakedness is a garment of love that He wears without shame.

Psalm 55:22 RSV
Cast your burden on the Lord, and he will sustain you; he will never permit the righteous to be moved.

REFLECTIONS

I hope you have a perfect day
in all you say and do.
And pray that your tomorrows
will reflect the life you choose.

And if all of those tomorrows
reflect a small part of your past,
I know the sun will shine
directly upon your chosen path.

Your path may be a little crooked
and it may climb a hill or two,
But according to your past
the Lord will walk with you.

Psalm 32:8 RSV
I will instruct you and teach you the way you should
go; I will counsel you with my eye upon you.

UNTIL THE SUN SMILES

We all have something special that will give us a sense of peace and contentment. Mine is when I open the doors and windows as a steady rain falls outside.

Sometimes opening the doors and windows makes the house feel on the cool side, but not cold. During that time, I curl up under a quilt with a good book. My cat will usually snuggle up next to me. I feel a sense of contentment knowing I am safe as I hear a clap of thunder rumbling across the sky.

During that special time, I feel that God has heard every word I have said to Him that day. As I watch the rain and listen to the thunder, I know that He cries when we cry and when we smile, He rejoices.

After the rain there will be a rainbow. And so, until the sun smiles upon my world, I will enjoy what I find before me.

Job 21:9 RSV
Their houses are safe from fear, and no rod of God is upon them.

TRUST ME

The years come, the years go.
And I find a soft warm glow
within my heart that won't depart.
Because I know you love me so.

If I cry and turn aside,
I know you'll always be there
to help me home.
No more to roam.

You'll care and share.
My burdens you will bear.
If I dare give them to you.
Because I know you love me so.

But do I dare?
Do I allow you to care?
and wipe away my pain?
Or do I take it back again?

Because you know I love you so,
what have you to gain
if you hold onto your pain?
Trust Me and let Me have your pain.

Psalm 56:4 KJV
In God I will praise his word, in God I have put my
trust; I will not fear what flesh can do unto me.

THE HAND OF GOD

I sat in a beautiful meadow. The grass was fresh and a breeze touched my brow. I saw a small rabbit on its way to some place that I did not know. I saw the beauty of wild flowers bending on the wind and my heart was touched by the beauty of all that was before me.

Suddenly I saw my friend in the distance. He came to me and sat down. We sat in silence for a few moments and then he said:

"There are many ways to touch the hand of God. Do not take lightly the little ways."

Thank you Lord for the little things in life. Amen.

Psalm 103:15-16 NAS
As for man, his days are like grass; As a flower of the field, so he flourishes. When the wind has passed over it, it is no more.

BECAUSE OF HIM

I feel as if I have been on a long journey. I have climbed some tough and rugged mountains. I have gone through dry deserts and I have crossed raging rivers. At times I felt as if I could not take another step. But throughout my journey I found a Friend that was willing to catch me when I began to fall from those mountains. He gave me drink and food in the deserts. He took my hand and He helped me cross those raging rivers. I know that if I should travel to the coldest part of the earth, He would keep me warm.

My Friend is my Lord Jesus Christ. Because of Him, I can see with new eyes. Yes, I can look out over the land before me and because of Him . . . I see Love.

John 1:16 NIV
From the fullness of his grace we have all received one blessing after another.

COME AND PLAY

The wind beckons me to come and play.
As it calls my name, I can feel its icy fingers
scratching upon my window and the terror I feel
draws me near. I do not dare walk into the wind
for I may not return.
But it waits until my guard is down and my
quietness returns. Then it sings a lullaby.
Waiting for me to sleep.
And sleep I long for . . . Forever.

Then a voice calls me to awaken and brilliance
disturbs my eyes. Warmth floods my being.
Birds sing outside my window.
The wind is gone and time casts a rainbow into
my life. I sing a song of joy.
I do not need to fear the wind. For its icy
fingers are not cold at all. They were merely
branches dancing to a tune and their joy could
not be contained.

Isaiah 41:10 KJV
Fear thou not; for I am with thee: be not dismayed;
for I am thy God: I will strengthen thee; yea, I will help
thee; yea, I will uphold thee with the right hand of my
righteousness.

JUSTICE

Malachi 2:17 RSV

You have wearied the Lord with your words. Yet you say, "How have we wearied him?" By saying, "Everyone who does evil is good in the sight of the Lord, and he delights in them." Or by asking, "Where is the God of justice?"

The first part of this scripture is very powerful and has a very powerful message, but I will wait to reflect on its message at another time. The part of the scripture above that comes to my attention today is the last sentence. "Where is the God of justice?" I must confess that I have found myself thinking the same question. There is so much sadness and so many things that seem to be wrong in our world today. I find myself asking the same question asked so many years ago. "Where is the God of justice?"

Actually, the first part of this scripture may be a reflection of the last question. If we view the beautiful garden created so many years ago, we cannot help but ask that same question another time.

As I sat reflecting on this question during my quiet time, I found myself repeating it several times. After I had repeated it three times, I thought I heard some words within my heart. I sat very quietly to see if I could hear them again. The words became clear. There was no way to mistake their meaning. The words I heard were:

"He's sitting by your side." No more needed to be said.

"Where is the God of justice?"
"He's sitting by your side."
Amen.

LOOKING RATHER FUNNY

One morning my cat wanted to look out of my bedroom window. As I sat with a cup of coffee in my hand, I watched him push and poke at the mini blind that was in his way. Finally he was able to sit on the window sill. But he did not look very comfortable because the mini blind sat on him in a very funny position.

As I walked over to where he sat, looking rather unhappy, I realized that we do the same thing in our own lives. We poke and push things, trying to get them to do what we want. We usually find ourselves looking rather funny and feeling very unhappy.

I lifted the mini blind from the cat's head. He seemed to say "Thank you" to me as he turned to watch the rain that was falling on the other side of the window.

Just as the cat allowed me to help him, we need to allow God into our days so that he can lift the mini blinds for us. Most importantly we need to remember to say "Thank You Lord" as we watch the rain fall on the other side of the window.

1 Chronicles 29:13 KJV
Now therefore, our God, we thank thee, and praise thy glorious name.

THE QUESTION

I walked on streets that were unfamiliar to me. I saw people that I did not know. A man in tattered clothing was talking with several men of stature. I could not hear what they were talking about and so I drew near to them. When I got close enough, I realized that the man in the tattered clothing had been blind and now he could see.

I then realized where I was. As I was about to say something to the men, I felt the presence of someone at my side. Turning, I saw a friend. He placed his hand upon my shoulder. He asked me a question. The question that he asked was the same one that the blind man had asked the men of stature. This was his question: "Do you too, want to become his disciple?"

My answer was quick and short. My answer was yes. In reply to my answer he said:

"Yes? Look closely. Will you be able to do all that the disciples have done? Will you be able to follow? Will you be able to pray? Will you argue between each other? Will you betray? Will you be able to forgive? Will you be able to go on and teach? Will you see Me in the eyes and hearts of others? Will you love Me?"

"Look closely. Do you too, want to become MY disciple?"

"If you must be perfect in all that you do . . . rethink the answer to My question. Do you **really** want to be My disciple?"

John 9:27 RSV

He answered them, "I have told you already, and you would not listen. Why do you want to hear it again? Do you too want to become his disciples?"

Sometimes you may not agree with what your family does, but continue to shower them with the love that Jesus has placed within you.... For if you love them with the love of Jesus.... you will also find love.

I am allowed to write things because God allows me to hear them in my heart, see them in my mind and know them in my soul. You do the same.

A DARK ROOM

I was in a meeting one day and we were discussing how we could allow God's love to enter our lives. As I sat listening, the following thoughts entered my mind.

When you are in a dark room and you open the door to another room filled with light, the light from that room will enter the darkness and the darkness will become light.

That is very true, but we can also enter the lighted room and render it dark. The choice is ours. We can live in the Light or we can survive in the dark.

We also have the choice to do the same thing for others. A kind word or a smile may bring light to someone and a frown may turn off a light.

I hope I can turn on a light for someone today.

Thank you Lord. Amen.

John 1:6-8 NRSV

There was a man sent from God, whose name was John. He came as a witness to testify to the light, so that all might believe through him. He himself was not the light, but he came to testify to the light.

BE CONTENT

I was walking with a friend. As we walked on a dusty road, I asked a question. This is his reply: "What is success? Is it being somebody to the whole world or being loved by those around you? If you can be content with those around you, you can be content with the world. Because those around you may be few or those around you may be many. So be content with those around you."

Psalm 118:25 NIV
O Lord, save us; O Lord, grant us success.

ALPHA AND OMEGA

I sat quietly. Within my heart I heard these words:
"The power of God is in many things.

It is in a seedling silently breaking through the crust of brown earth.

The wind as it comes and goes.

The purring of a kitten.

Children as they explore the beauty of the world around them.

An artist's picture or a sculptor's masterpiece.

A typewriter tapping words of concern.

The trees bursting into glorious beauty after a winter sleep.

Clouds floating gracefully in uncharted skies.

A smile received unexpectedly. And you.

The power of God is within you because God loves you. The power of God is within you because you can choose to love others.

Give to others what you want for yourself. Give freely . . . without restrictions. Because with restrictions, you also will be restricted. If you give with only yourself in mind then you will find only yourself at the end of your endeavor.

I must be first and then you will find Me at the end also. I am the beginning and the end. The Alpha and Omega."

I understand Lord.

Thank you for all that you have given to me. I know this is true for all of us. Amen.

Revelation 1:8 NIV

"I am the Alpha and the Omega," says the Lord God, "who is, and who was, and who is to come, the Almighty."

DANCING WITH THE SUN

There's a sunbeam in my kitchen.
I like to make it laugh.
When I touch its shining rays,
It dances in my path.

It makes me smile with such delight.
A child I then become.
Because the child within my heart
Is dancing with the sun.

Psalm 149:3 KJV
Let them praise his name in the dance: let them sing praises unto him with the timbrel and harp.

GOD'S LOVE

When it rains upon the prairie
And flowers begin to bloom.
You can see God's handiwork
Within a silver moon.

Yes, spring comes to the prairie
With birds that take to flight.
And sounds are heard abundantly
Within a starry night.

To see such beauty within our world
Is something to behold.
When spring comes to the prairie
God's love is there to hold.

Joel 2:22 RSV
Fear not, you beasts of the field, for the pastures of the wilderness are green: the tree bears its fruit, the fig tree and vine give their full yield.

ROSES

I was in a room with the shades closed. It was dark and the room made me feel sad. I turned to leave the room when a friend joined me. He looked around the room and said:

"If you do not open the shades, you will not see that which is beyond and you will not be aware of the roses that await you."

See the roses bright with color. You are one.
One with another.
See the roses in varying color. The sun shines on one.
One shines on another.
See the roses on the same vine. They grow in time.
Time is the vine.
The roses are Mine.
The roses are Mine. I tend them each day.
The roses are Mine until time passes away.
Their color may fade. Their fragrances depart.
The roses are Mine and they're still in my heart.
My heart's safe and warm. The sun always shines.
The roses are safe. The roses are Mine.

2 Corinthians 2:15-16 RSV
For we are the aroma of Christ to God among those who are being saved and among those who are perishing, to one a fragrance from death to death, to the other a fragrance from life to life....

IN MY HOME

I approached a small house that stood beside a quiet river. I could see the curtains blowing in the wind and I could smell the flowers that were lovingly placed along the path that led to the gate. The gate had a sign that welcomed the weary traveler that walked the dusty road. As I stood before the open gate, I saw a friend in the door of the little house. He waved and motioned for me to join him. He put his arm around me and said:

"You are always welcome in my humble home . . . no matter where your feet have taken you. If they have walked where kings have walked, you are welcome in my home. If they have walked where no one should walk, you are welcome here with me. If they have walked where you and I now walk, we will walk together."

"In my home . . . **all** are welcome."

John 4:6 KJV
Now Jacob's well was there. Jesus therefore, being wearied with his journey, sat thus on the well: and it was about the sixth hour.

THE ANGELS ARE NEAR

I know the angels are near me today.
I can hear their voices. I hear what they say.

They are here to show me a child that is blessed.
A child that came to give me some rest.

They are here to tell me of a Savior Divine.
They are here to show me the path that is mine.

A path that leads to a stable in time.
They show me a child. Our Savior Divine.

The angels are near me. I feel all their love.
The angels were sent from heaven above.

Yes, I bow low in wonder. I bow low in awe.
Thinking about the baby I saw.
He touched my heart as well as my mind.
That tiny baby . . . My Savior Divine.

Luke 2:10-11 RSV
And the angel said to them, "Be not afraid; for behold, I bring you good news of a great joy which will come to all the people; for to you is born this day in the city of David a Savior, who is Christ the Lord."

A NEW COMMANDMENT

I was reading Exodus 20:1-17. This part of Exodus gives us the Ten Commandments. Sometimes I feel so inadequate in keeping all of the Commandments. I often feel a twinge of guilt because I feel that I have let the Lord down in those areas.

As I read the scripture, I said this prayer: "Lord; I strive to keep Your commandments. Forgive me if I fail even one. Amen."

Within my heart I felt that He spoke these words to me:

"My child, I have given you a new commandment. If you strive to keep that one commandment the others will be done."

Thank you Lord for Your Commandments. Amen.

John 13:34 RSV
A new commandment I give to you, that you love one another; even as I have loved you, that you also love one another.

YOU ARE MY BRANCHES

As I sat reflecting upon the sadness that I felt when a friend moved away, I heard the following words within my heart:

"I am the vine. You are the branches."

"Have you ever watched a vine grow? It reaches out. It spreads and can cover a large area. It reaches farther and farther. Even when it has no place to cling . . . it continues to reach out."

"If too many branches are left in one area, they can become tangled within each other. They can hinder the growth of each other and so, I gently separate each part of the vine to allow their growth. That they may continue to grow and not become tangled. My branches must continue to reach out and cover the entire world with green leaves."

"If one leaf becomes yellow, it is removed. Remember, over watering causes yellow leaves and under watering allows the same yellowness. It is not easy. A balance for each plant is needed."

"I am the vine. You are My branches."

John 15:1-2 RSV
"I AM the true vine, and my Father is the vinedresser. Every branch of mine that bears no fruit, he takes away, and every branch that does bear fruit he prunes, that it may bear more fruit."

WHY?

I looked into His face so dear.
Then I noticed all His tears.

I stopped my asking, "Why, oh why?"
And dried the tears within His eyes.

He looked at me and said, "Don't cry."
And dried the tears within my eyes.

I began to smile the best I could.
It's then I knew He understood.

John 11:35 KJV
    Jesus wept.

CRYSTAL TEARS

I came to the cross and knelt to pray.

I saw your feet as I knelt to pray. They were dusty from the road you were asked to walk. As I knelt, the blood from your crown was felt on my brow and I felt the pain you quietly held. Through that one drop of blood I felt the pain of the entire world for centuries and it hurt. But you said it was all right because you loved us.

They took you down and carried you away. They laid you on a roughly carved rock. Your arms fell limp and they were gently laid at your side. You were anointed with oil and tenderly covered with a linen cloth.

I cried for you that day. I wanted to say so much. I wanted you to know how much I loved you for doing this for me. But I couldn't say a word.

My tears streamed down my cheeks and splashed upon your pure linen cloth. I did not notice my tears that day as they lay at your feet.

I was led away by others who mourned. They shared my grief in the middle of a storm.

As we walked away, you could see us go. We were not a pretty sight. We wept and moaned in sorrow and grief. Then you noticed the tears at your feet. You picked one up and placed it in your hand. You looked at me and said, "I understand."

They say my tears turned to crystal that day. The Lord took them with Him and they are sacred today.

Go to the cross and kneel at His feet. Your tears will turn to crystal as they are laid at His feet.

John 20:11-13 RSV

But Mary stood weeping outside the tomb, and as she wept she stooped to look into the tomb; and she saw two angels in white, sitting where the body of Jesus had lain, one at the head and one at the feet. They said to her, "Woman, why are you weeping?"

A CHINA DOLL

I have a friend that reminds me of a beautiful China doll placed upon a shelf. As I gaze upon her, I know that she has been placed so high that I am unable to reach those heights.

If I should get a stool to stand upon, I could probably see her more closely. But then, I may want to touch her and if I should touch her, I might drop her. If that should happen, the pieces would scatter across the floor before me and I might find out that she is human.

I will allow that beautiful China doll to sit upon the shelf . . . knowing one day I can probably hold her and say "I love you."

Song of Solomon 6:9 RSV

My dove, my perfect one, is only one, the darling of her mother, flawless to her that bore her. The maidens saw her and called her happy: the queens and concubines also, and they praised her.

YOUR GUARDIAN ANGEL

I sat praying for a friend. As I prayed, I heard these words within my heart:

I am not an eagle, but I soar with majestic wings.
I see with eyes of a centurion.
I represent grace and beauty.
My wings spread to the ends of the earth and I climb to great heights . . . beyond the stars and the moon.
I am as gentle as the butterfly within the palm of your hand.
I protect you by day and by night.
I befriend you.
I listen to you in joy . . . and in sorrow.
I love you as no one else can love you.
I am your Guardian Angel and I am with you always. Amen.

I feel this little poem might have a special message for a friend of mine. I hope she enjoys it. By the way, I like the thought of a Guardian Angel. How about you?

Psalm 91:11 RSV
For he will give his angels charge of you to guard you in all your ways.

HE CRIES

I felt a friend's arm around my shoulder. He spoke to me as I gazed upon the cross. I heard him say these words:

"Jesus is felt in a gentle breeze, but He is in the thunder also. He walks in the desert and He calms the mighty sea. The earth produces nourishment and the skies offer life. Beauty is seen within the palm of His hand and in the other . . . He cries over the darkness of His children."

Forgive us Lord. Amen.

Acts 26:18 KJV
To open their eyes, and to turn them from darkness to light, and from the power of Satan unto God, that they may receive forgiveness of sins, and inheritance among them which are sanctified by faith that is in me.

YOU'RE LOOKING AT ME

All I can do is hold you close.
And give you strength when you need it most.

I'll put my arms around you each day.
I hear your thoughts when you stop and pray.

I'll take your hand and help you to see.
When you look at them, you're looking at Me.

To show them your love is hard I know.
But you are a seed I've chosen to sow.

Within each garden there are some weeds.
To avoid their thorns stay close to Me.

Know that I love you as you love Me.
When they look at you, they look at Me.

1 John 4:7 KJV
   *Beloved, let us love one another: for love is of God;
and every one that loveth is born of God, and knoweth
God.*

SILVER AND GOLD

There is silver and gold
in all that we do.
There are medals in heaven
for those who are true.

We may not hold medals
in our hands as we live.
But there is silver and gold
in all those who give.

The silver is shown
in so many ways.
The gold reflects
in words that we say.

As treasures are shared
with others in need,
The medals we hold
are people we see.

Proverbs 25:11 NAS
   *Like apples of gold in settings of silver is a word
spoken in right circumstances.*

ON THE ROAD
TO EMMAUS

A man approached me as I walked a dusty road. He joined me as I walked trudgingly. He seemed to have no problem walking, so I said, "sir, would you be willing to exchange your feet for mine?"

The man gently, without words, slipped out of his sandals. It was then that I noticed the holes in his feet. I said, "I'm sorry, but I'm unable to exchange my feet for yours. Your feet look as if I would have more problems walking on them than you do."

He quietly slipped into his sandals and began to walk away. I watched him for a moment and then I suddenly ran to him. As I tugged at his garment, he turned to face me. I said, "I'm sorry that I was unable to exchange my feet for yours, but maybe I could exchange my hands."

As he unfolded his hands from the prayer he was saying, I noticed the holes in his hands. "I'm sorry." I said. "I cannot exchange my hands for yours. They look as if I might not be able to hold close those things that I see as important to me."

The man folded his hands and walked on. I watched him once more and then ran to catch him as he began to round a curve. "Though I am unable to exchange feet and hands with you, will you exchange hats with me? Mine will give you shade in order for you to have a comfortable journey."

The man quietly removed his hat. I noticed the wounds upon his brow and said, "I'm sorry, I cannot exchange hats with you. Yours carries too much pain."

The man had remained silent until now and as he looked at me he said, "Maybe another day you will be able to join me on my road. Maybe later you will be able to wear my clothes."

The man turned and as I quietly said, "Forgive me." He walked into the sun filled sky.

Luke 24:13-16 NRSV

Now on that same day two of them were going to a village called Emmaus, about seven miles from Jerusalem, and talking with each other about all these things that had happened. While they were talking and discussing, Jesus himself came near and went with them, but their eyes were kept from recognizing him.

A TINY BABY

The cry of a Savior
Rang loud and clear.
It rang through the heavens
For the world to hear.

A tiny baby
Born in the night.
This tiny baby
Brought the world light.

His birth is remembered
From year to year.
The cry of a Savior
The world did hear.

Matthew 2:1-2 KJV
Now when Jesus was born in Bethlehem of Judea in the days of Herod the king, behold, there came wise men from the east to Jerusalem, saying, "Where is he that is born King of the Jews? For we have seen his star in the east, and are come to worship him.

PATCHES AND POCKETS

Patches and pockets
Whatnot and such.
So often we mend
The hearts that we touch.

They're broken and bruised.
They're tattered and torn.
So often they sulk
And cry so forlorn.

They reach out to others
With threads loose and bare.
Hoping their hearts
Will show that they dare.

So mend those hearts slowly
With patience and care.
The hearts that we touch
Then life they can bear.

Psalm 147:3 RSV
He heals the brokenhearted, and binds up their wounds.

FRIENDSHIP

Friends are like gifts.

They come in many shapes, sizes, colors and with assorted bows. But each one is very special. Each one is as delicate as a rose. As true friendship grows and their petals begin to open, the inner beauty of the gift is allowed to show. For only with true friendship is this process allowed to happen. With true friendship we can show who we really are. We are willing to risk opening our petals to full bloom and we allow our inner beauty to be seen. The beauty is special. The friendship clear. The gift is forever. For both to hold dear.

2 Corinthians 9:15 RSV
   Thanks be to God for his inexpressible gift!

KNOWLEDGE

You are the hands of Christ.
He reaches no farther than you reach.
You are the feet of Christ.
He walks no farther than you walk.
You are the eyes of Christ.
He sees no farther than you see.
You are the voice of Christ.
He says no more than what you say.
You are the love of Christ.
How will you share it?
You are the body of Christ.
What will each of you choose to do?
With such knowledge?

Psalm 26:3 KJV
For thy lovingkindness is before mine eyes: and I have walked in thy truth.

EASTER SUNDAY

The small child was lifted by her mother from the communion rail. In her small hand she held a communion cup. With an insistent voice we could hear her say: "I want more!"

It was Easter Sunday. What more could have been said that day?

Yes, He has risen!

Just as the child exclaimed "I want more!" I pray that each of us will say the same. Amen.

Luke 24:50-51 RSV

Then he led them out as far as Bethany, and lifting up his hands he blessed them. While he blessed them, he parted from them, and was carried up into heaven.